MW01516478

GARIBALDI SENIOR SECONDARY
24789 Dewdney Trunk Road
Maple Ridge, B.C. V4R

Making FRIENDS, Finding LOVE

Making
FRIENDS,
Finding
LOVE

Julie Tallard Johnson

Lerner Publications Company • Minneapolis

LIBRARY OF CONGRESS CATALOGING-IN-PUBLICATION DATA

Johnson, Julie Tallard.
   Making friends, finding love : a book about teen relationships /
Julie Tallard Johnson.
      p.   cm.
   Includes bibliographical references and index.
   Summary: Provides advice about building friendships and romances,
discussing family relationships, sexual intimacy, jealousy, and
other topics.
   ISBN 0-8225-0045-0
   1. Interpersonal relations in adolescence—Juvenile literature.
2. Interpersonal relations in adolescence—Case studies—Juvenile
literature. [1. Friendship. 2. Interpersonal relations.]
I. Title.
BF724.3.I58J64   1992
158'.2'0835—dc20   91-40792
                                                                  CIP
                                                                   AC

Manufactured in the United States of America

1 2 3 4 5 6 7 8 9 10 01 00 99 98 97 96 95 94 93 92

Author's Note

Not only have my friendships helped me get through insecure and difficult times, but they have significantly added to my life. In fact, my friendships are some of the greatest gifts I have been given. My friendships have also offered me lessons that have contributed to who I am. Tommy Engelbrecht taught me one of my most treasured lessons.

When I was between the ages of two and four, Tommy lived two houses down from me. We were inseparable. We played side by side. Since I lived in a family with four other children for my mother to care for, Tommy's company was vital to my sense of security and love. Sadly, about the time I turned five, Tommy moved to the other side of town. I lost my best friend.

Later, when I entered sixth grade, there he was again. Eight years had passed, but our friendship seemed to continue where it had left off. Once again, we were inseparable. But certain cultural expectations of the time began to affect us: my teacher called me "boy crazy" because my best friend was a boy. Other kids would tease us about being "sweethearts." Regardless of such pressures, we remained friends throughout sixth grade and the following summer.

It was in the beginning of the seventh grade that I gave in to the belief that "girls and boys cannot be 'just friends.'" Tommy and I talked one day about whether or not we could be girlfriend and boyfriend and decided we couldn't be. It seemed at the time that friendship wasn't an option either. Regretfully, I decided to allow the friendship to end because everyone thought we were boyfriend and girlfriend, and we were not. In addition, we were moving among different groups of friends. So Tommy and I parted ways. Since it was a large school and we belonged to different groups, our paths never crossed again.

The lesson I learned much later was not to let other people's rules or biases dictate my friendships; all cultural and family expectations are not automatically correct. One of my best friends today is a man. I also learned not to let stereotypes and real or perceived differences keep me from a meaningful relationship.

There are times when I find myself missing Tommy.

*This book is most affectionately
dedicated to my pen pal, Charlene.*

CONTENTS

Introduction by Anna Christine Swanson   9

1 *Friendships*   11

2 *Ending Loneliness*   22

3 *Family Relationships*   30

4 *Finding Love*   41

5 *Setting Limits in Relationships*   52

6 *When It's Time to Say Good-Bye*   59

For Further Reading   63

Index   64

INTRODUCTION

When I was about nine years old, my parents got divorced. At the time, it didn't mean much to me—I just went on being a kid. As I got older and my parents began to have new relationships, however, many feelings began to surface. I felt alone, sad, scared, and helpless. Where once my family relationships had been understandable and predictable, now everything was changing. If it weren't for my parents' love for me, I'm not sure how I would have gotten through these years.

With their help I began to understand that even though they had other relationships, I still had a family I could turn to. They still loved me. I discovered that I had many reasons to be happy and that I wasn't helpless. I'm still not totally accustomed to the divorce. It's hard for me to accept that there is someone else in my parents' lives besides one another. Even though other families have experienced divorce, none of my close friends come from divorced families. This makes it harder for me. But I also realize that divorce isn't the only challenge we face as teens and families.

I have a friend who hates the holidays because her parents' families are always fighting. Her holidays are a long series of arguments. Even though my parents are divorced, holidays are one of my favorite times, because we all get together and share a lot of love and fun. One thing that has really helped me is that my parents have always worked things out with each other. I know that they divorced each other, not me.

Now, at the age of 17, I am learning many lessons through my peer relationships. I have not yet had a steady boyfriend. This used to really bother me. I wondered what was wrong with me. I thought if I could only change my personality enough, someone would like me. By talking this over with my parents, reading Julie's book, and through experience, I know it doesn't work to try to change myself to get someone to accept me. Trying to force someone to like me only left me frustrated and hurt. Now if someone wants me to be his boyfriend, he will have to like me for who I am.

I have learned as a teenager that friendships can be difficult but worthwhile. Because we are all changing so much, we drift apart or get involved with different people. I sometimes worry about not having a lasting friendship or about getting a divorce after I am married. Still, even though relationships are risky and can be painful, each one of mine has been worthwhile and has given me something new and helpful.

I'm glad Julie has written this book on teen relationships, because she is willing to touch on topics that many adults and teens find hard to talk about openly. Although getting into a relationship with someone may mean it will end someday, having relationships is, after all, what life is all about.

Anna Christine Swanson, age 17

CHAPTER ONE

Friendships

Betsi and I are best friends. We do everything together. She knows me better than anyone, even my parents.

Annette, age 15

This world seems like a war zone of drugs, pollution, angry parents, racism—if it weren't for my friend Tony, I would probably be dead.

Stephen, age 17

Friendships are a major part of our lives. During our young adult years (ages 13 to 25), friendships often become our key relationships. Friendships, unlike young adult romances, tend to last many years.

I live in a small tourist town where new boys hang out all summer. It can be fun dating these guys and spending the summer with them. But I learned the first time I fell in love with one of these boys that boyfriends come and go, but my friends remain forever.

Cayce, age 17

Friendships grow as you and your friends discover more and more about each other. Some friendships will be short-lived, like when you make a friend at camp or on vacation; others will last a lifetime. Throughout our lives, our friendships change, but our need for friends remains constant.

During our teen years, friendships are usually quite intense and meaningful. Later our relationships with spouses, partners, or families may become primary, but for most teenagers, making and keeping friends is very important.

Most days I think Lee and I are friends, but sometimes I really wonder. Does she stick up for me when others are talking about me? Does she consider me one of her best friends? She's more popular than me and I'm not so sure if she always likes me.

Tamara, age 15

Billy and I were best friends in the eighth grade. We did everything together. Our families are good friends, too. But now that I'm in the ninth grade it seems like we have different interests. It's hard to hang out with more than one group—it's like you have to choose or be left out. I really like Billy and I'm not sure what I'm going to do.

Zenon, age 16

Everyone on my basketball team is my friend. I'm not sure what I'll do if I don't make the team next year.

Keith, age 16

I don't really have any close friends. I think people are embarrassed to hang out with me because I have so much acne.

Elliott, age 15

All my friends are in wheelchairs like me. I would like to have at least one friend who isn't disabled.

Alex, age 17

One thing's certain about teen relationships—nothing feels too certain. Although relationships at this time in your life can be confusing and scary, your teenage years are a good time to explore the possibilities close friendships can offer you. Marriage, long-term commitments, and career choices are approaching but are not yet priorities. As you prepare for adult independence, you can take time to explore various interests, enjoy many different people and experiences, and build your self-esteem.

I met Andrea in seventh-grade art class. I was searching for a friend—a best friend. We started to talk and I felt instantly that we could be good friends. She was interested in what I had to say and I was excited about getting to know more about her. For about three years we were very close; we did nearly everything together. We've gone through many changes in our lives since then, yet 20 years later we remain friends. It is Andrea's respect and love for who I am, and mine for who she is, that keep our friendship alive. She is still as interested in what I am doing, what I think about, and how I feel, as she was that first day we met in seventh-grade art class.

Marnie, age 35

It was hard being friends with Barbara. No matter what I did, I never felt connected or happy about our relationship. I was always there when she needed me, and it turned out she needed me often to help her out of some situation. For a while it felt good to be needed but that feeling didn't last long. It wasn't until about 10 years later that I realized whenever it came her turn to help me, she wasn't able to for some reason or other. I finally decided that I had given enough to this relationship and said my good-byes to her in a letter after she moved to California. Even though I felt sad to say good-bye, I wasn't really letting go of a friend.

Ruth, age 27

There is a great difference between what Marnie and Ruth experienced in their respective friendships. Like them, you will learn many valuable lessons in your teen and adult relationships. One of these lessons is a gradual understanding of who makes a good friend for you and who does not.

Although friendships often seem to happen naturally, all friendships are full of twists and turns that can be challenging and painful. Relationships do not happen by accident—you choose your friends. You have control over whom you become friends with and whom you choose not to be friends with. Ideally, friendship is the foundation of all relationships. But what is a friend? And what goes into a friendship?

Creating a good friendship takes energy, time, and involvement. Learning to make and keep friends requires skill and effort. Making friends may be easy or difficult for you. If friendships are hard for you, this does not mean you are a bad person or unlikeable. It simply means you need to learn the skills—the ingredients—necessary to create healthy friendships.

What Makes a Friendship?

A friend is someone who likes a lot of the same things I do.

Peter, age 13

A friend is someone I can talk with about *anything*.

Claire, age 16

My friends help keep me sober.

Kenrick, age 19

One way to think about creating a friendship is that it's like following a recipe, such as a recipe for an omelette. Omelettes are easy to make if you know the recipe and have the right ingredients and utensils. Various items are needed to cook an omelette (and not everyone makes one exactly the same way). Like most skills, cooking comes more naturally with time and practice. Somebody probably taught you how to cook and allowed you to make mistakes. It's the same with friendship: give yourself and others the patience and kindness to learn "how to make" a healthy friendship. Find out what is needed to make a good friendship, and allow yourself and your friends to make mistakes. Here are some of the "ingredients" that go into a friendship.

Ingredient one: Be a friend to yourself first. How do you treat yourself? Others tend to treat us as we treat ourselves. You don't have to be perfect to be a friend. The kinder you are to yourself, however, the kinder your friends will be to you.

Like all our relationships, friendships tell us something about ourselves. A friendship is like a mirror. Whom you choose as a friend says a lot about how you feel about yourself. What are your mirrors telling you? Do you like what you see?

As an exercise, list all the characteristics that bother you about a particular friend. For example, you may be dating someone who always shows up late and sometimes forgets your dates altogether. Or maybe you have a friend who gossips about others, rarely saying anything good about them. Jennifer, age 19, describes a friend who "never calls me—I always have to call her if I want to get together to do something."

Next, ask yourself what these characteristics may say about you. The way you allow others to treat you says something about you. What might it mean about Jennifer that she always calls her friend but her friend never calls her? This is what Jennifer discovered:

> I realized that I had *let* others treat me a certain way. I couldn't change anyone else, but I could change myself. I started to let more people know what I wanted and expected from them. A few people got mad at me, but most didn't realize anything bothered me until I told them. I was scared to speak up, but it's better than being treated poorly by others.

What is your mirror telling you? Make a list of all the characteristics you enjoy about a friend and then think about what this says about you as well.

Ingredient two: Trust. Everyone wants—and needs—to trust others. But trusting others does not mean blindly giving yourself over to someone or doing things you don't want to do. Trust is something others *earn*, not something you give away freely.

How can you know who is trustworthy and who is not? This question is challenging. You don't have to jump into a relationship; give yourself time to get to know someone. When the person is able to follow through on the smaller expectations and commitments of a friendship, extend more trust.

Before you begin to trust someone, consider what is important to you in a friend or partner. Is she reliable?

Does he follow through on his promises? How does this person treat others? If someone is reliable, for example, it is probably safe to trust a bit more. Remember, both people contribute to the feeling of trust in a relationship. You need to be reliable and considerate of your friend, too.

Ingredient three: Honesty. Honesty means more than just not lying. Honesty includes being open with others about your feelings, beliefs, and desires. Consistently let others know how you feel and what you want. Be honest with yourself and others about your beliefs.

Ingredient four: Availability. Being available for your friend means being consistent and reliable. A person who is consistent is willing to spend time with you regularly and relates to you in a predictable way. He doesn't show up sulky and short-tempered one day, apologetic the next day, and angry with you the day after that. Some fluctuations in others' personalities are natural, but it is fair to expect a certain degree of consistency from your friends.

Being reliable means that when you (or someone else) make a commitment, you follow through with it. If you ask someone to keep Saturday night open for you, for example, you do not turn around and make plans with someone else that night. If you can't make your date, let the other person know as soon as you can so she can make other plans.

If someone only wants to see you when it is convenient for her, and she is not willing to be there when you need her, the friendship lacks availability. Availability also means being emotionally supportive. When you feel sad, your friend respects your feeling and either comforts you or simply allows you to be sad. Your friend is aware of and accepts your moods.

Availability means that both friends focus their attention on the relationship and what's happening when they're together. Have you ever spent time with someone who seems preoccupied with other events or people?

> I have a friend who always reminds me of what she did with so-and-so. . . . If she has already been to the place we are visiting, she talks on and on about what a good time she had *last* time. Just once I would like to hear about how much fun she is having with me, right now. I feel so unimportant compared to the others.
>
> MaryAnne, age 18

Keeping your attention and energy focused on the present moment allows you to enjoy more fully the person you are with and the experience you are sharing.

Ingredient five: Safety. In a safe relationship, both friends feel a deep respect and concern for each other's well-being. Friends do not hurt or neglect one another. Furthermore, in a safe relationship no one is asked to keep harmful secrets. For example, if you tell someone not to let others know that you are addicted to cocaine or that your boyfriend beat you up, you're asking your friend to keep a harmful secret.

Relationships become unsafe when you feel pressured to act in a way that is not in your best interest. A relationship is unsafe, for example, if a friend pressures you to use drugs, if your boyfriend hits you, or if your friend asks you to lie to your parents about what you did over the weekend.

In abusive relationships, secrets can keep the abuse or problem from being stopped: "Don't tell anyone that I hit you or I'll really hurt you next time"; "Stop complaining about Mom's drinking—the whole world doesn't have to know what you think"; "If you are really my friend, you won't tell anyone that my nosebleed is because of cocaine." Threats are never part of any safe relationship. If someone has to threaten you to keep a secret or stay in a relationship, the relationship is dangerous.

Ingredient six: Love. You don't have to wait until you are in a romantic partnership with someone to experience love. Love is an important part of friendships, too. Love is a feeling of deep respect and fondness. A friend shows his or her love by treating you as a unique person with special qualities.

Ingredient seven: Respect. Respect for another's feelings and individuality is part of a healthy friendship. A friend will acknowledge and respect your differences without trying to change you.

> Lou and I strongly disagree on whether or not women should be able to have an abortion. This disagreement almost cost us our friendship. But then I realized that Lou has her reasons for believing what she does. It doesn't have to get in our way. Isn't that what friendship is all about—the freedom to express different opinions and still be liked? Our friendship was strong enough to withstand some differences.
>
> Annette, age 19

Ingredient eight: Reciprocity. In a healthy friendship, the give-and-take is balanced. This balance is reciprocity. What you give is not always the same as what you receive, however.

> My friendship with the lady down the block is me mostly listening to her stories and sometimes helping her mow her

lawn. She can't really do very much but sit around and talk. She has a lot to talk about, though. She tells me about the people who used to live in all the houses. She's lived here over 35 years, longer than anyone else on the block. I get a lot from my visits with her.

Craig, age 18

Relationships are built on equality and reciprocity. As Craig's story shows, equality and reciprocity come in a variety of forms. Unequal, nonreciprocal relationships are at best boring and at worst abusive. If you are not getting anything from a friendship, be willing to let the person go.

I was in a relationship for a long time where I gave gifts, remembered her birthdays, sent her cards, asked her over, but she never offered me one gift or invited me over to her house to stay a night. I wish I had asked her why she didn't ask me to stay over or why she never gave me a card or gift, but I thought that was too pushy. I just stopped calling her and she never called me back. I see her sometimes at school. All she does is say hi, like nothing's different. I hope I have the courage to be more honest next time and ask someone why they are treating me a certain way. With her I'll never know.

Rachel, age 19

Ingredient nine: Growth. A healthy friendship changes and grows—it's dynamic. The way we know something is alive is that it is growing and changing constantly. A dead tree does not grow or respond to the seasons. A relationship needs to be alive with growth, too. A healthy friendship will encourage your personal growth and allow both friends to experiment safely with new ideas and experiences. Your friend may mature physically or start dating sooner than you, but this need not hurt your friendship. Hopefully, you can talk to each other about the many changes you are both experiencing and appreciate your differences.

All of the "ingredients" listed in this chapter are important in a healthy friendship. You have the right to expect these qualities in all your relationships, and others have the right to expect them from you. Be patient with yourself and others, however, as you learn about the dynamics of friendships. We all make mistakes as we continue to learn about ourselves throughout our lives.

CHAPTER TWO

Ending Loneliness

What if you have moved to a new city recently and haven't made any friends? Or what if you are shy and uncertain about meeting people? Some teens consider themselves unpopular and give up trying to make friends. Whoever you are, whatever your circumstances—whether you are disabled, shy, overweight, athletic, or wealthy—you need friends. Chances are you encounter at least a half-dozen people each day who are also searching for friends.

If you are lonely, how can you reach out to others and make friends? How can you become more popular, if this is what you want? A first step toward overcoming loneliness is to become better aware of *why* and *how* you are lonely.

Take a couple of minutes to describe your loneliness. This is what Jessica wrote about her loneliness and how it made her feel.

I live in the country, on a dairy farm, 10 miles away from the next family and 18 miles from school. I'm lonely because it takes over half an hour to get to and from school on the bus. I have no time for activities and groups after school, since I help my mother every night with dinner. And what fun would it be to invite anyone out to the farm? Most of the kids at school live in town. I bet the kids hate cow farms! I'm different from almost everyone in my class and I hate it.

What seem to be the causes of Jessica's loneliness? Does she assume anything that might not be true? How could she overcome her loneliness and isolation?

Here are three solutions that Jessica and her school counselor came up with:

1. Jessica will ask two girls in her English class out to the farm for a Saturday afternoon, even though it's far.
2. She will talk to at least one other teenager on the bus during her ride home from school, instead of reading a magazine or book.
3. She will ask her mother if her brother could help with dinner one night a week so she can join one of the after-school activities. Her counselor will help arrange for Jessica to get a ride home.

Now take some time to come up with at least three possible solutions to your own loneliness. You may want to get help from your school counselor or your parents. Remember to make the solutions *easy* and *immediate*—steps you can begin tomorrow. Some teens have found it helpful to write in a journal about their loneliness.

It's No Fun Being Shy

Loneliness often results from shyness. If you're shy, people often misjudge you as unfriendly or uninterested.

Everyone thinks I'm rude because I don't speak up much or make a lot of jokes. I'm considered athletic and attractive so others just assume I'm confident and clever. But I'm not! I hate trying to be funny, and groups of people make me real nervous. I get intensely shy around people, especially when attention is drawn to me. I just clam up, my throat gets real tight, and I start to sweat and turn red. Sometimes I feel like I could throw up. I'll not attend parties I was invited to—so the girl who invited me thinks I don't like her and the guys think I'm a jerk.

Dennis, age 17

The best cure for shyness and the loneliness that goes with it is to be willing to try new activities—even though doing them might make you feel anxious at first. You can overcome shyness by doing whatever scares you, over and over, until it becomes easier and easier for you. One way to start is to make a short list of times when you feel shy and nervous. You can use Dennis's list as an example:

The things that really make me anxious and shy are:

▲ when my parents ask me to do something in front of their friends, such as show off my athletic abilities, or when they brag about me while I'm standing there;

▲ parties, especially those where there are a lot of girls;

▲ groups of people in the school hallway or in classes, because I hate having to speak to a whole group;

▲ being expected to speak up in class. It often seems as if the teachers pick me more often than others in the class—like I enjoy getting so much attention!

Then, as Dennis does below, write out a new way you will

respond to at least two of the situations you listed. Dennis came up with the following:

▲ I will approach at least one group of friends in the hallway each day. I won't pressure myself to say more than hello. I'll talk about things I want to talk about and won't force myself to be clever or funny, unless something just comes to me.

▲ I'll go to one party this semester with my friend Bob, who knows how uncomfortable I am but doesn't pressure me about it. I'll consider approaching more of the girls just for conversation but won't force myself if I get too uncomfortable.

You might think of only one action or behavior to change —that's a fantastic start. When we want to change something about ourselves, such as shyness or loneliness, it takes many small steps to accomplish our goals. Two months after Dennis began working on his shyness, he had this to say:

I still get real nervous when I approach a group of people, but just hanging out for a while I find I get more and more relaxed. People don't expect me to be clever or talkative all the time, and that's a big relief. I also talked to my parents about not embarrassing me in front of their friends. They were real cool about it. Even though they still brag about me, they do less of it and they don't ask me to perform in front of their friends anymore.

Quick but Dangerous Relief
One way some teens and adults cope with their shyness is by using alcohol or drugs. Although alcohol may provide

immediate relief, it is only temporary. The alcohol may give you a sense of confidence for a time, but when it wears off nothing has changed. Relying on alcohol or drugs at social events can lead to a serious addiction. Although it might be uncomfortable to attend a social event sober if you're shy, you will gradually gain real confidence—not the false confidence drinking gives you.

When You Meet Someone You Like

Most people feel shy at one time or another. It's natural to be shy about getting to know someone or making new friends. You aren't sure how a new person will respond to you. What do you do when you want an acquaintance to turn into a friend, or you simply want to make more friends? How do you approach others?

> I'm not sure who to approach or how! I'm sure I'm gay, but it's real hard knowing who else might be. I'd sure like to be friends with other gay teens.
>
> Aleck, age 17

> I was sure she liked me too, but I was petrified when I thought of approaching her. So I left a note in her locker that expressed my interest in her. She then left me a note with her phone number. Now I'm scared to call her.
>
> Davis, age 16

When you approach someone new, you run the risk of being rejected. But without taking the risk, you miss out on the opportunity to get to know someone better. The longer you wait to express your interest in someone, the more nervous you tend to become. If you're interested in someone, take the risk and call him or her before you build up too much fear about doing it. The worst that can happen is that the person will say no—and we have all survived disappointments. Most people will take your interest in them as a compliment.

When you aren't sure about what kind of activity to do when you get together with a new friend, choose something you think you will both enjoy. This could be an activity that the other person is experienced in and that is new for you. For example, maybe your new friend can show you how to rollerblade, introduce you to the state fair, or show you her art projects. Next you can introduce the person to one of your favorite activities. Or you could go to a movie or sporting event together.

During the early stages of a friendship, you and the other person are exploring whether or not you enjoy each other's company and want to continue getting together. During this time in a friendship—or a romance, for that matter—take time to find out about one another. What are the other person's interests, likes, and dislikes?

Try not to push the friendship along too fast. Give yourself time to discover whether this person is a good friend for you. Enjoy this time of your friendship, regardless of how it develops. Have fun—playfulness is an important part of every relationship.

When you find yourself liking this person more and more, let him know about your feelings. If you would like to spend more time together, tell him you look forward to getting together again soon. Be honest about your feelings.

Most importantly, *be yourself*. The best friendships are built by two people who stay true to their beliefs, values, and needs. If you feel you must change something about yourself to win someone's friendship, that friendship is too costly. Don't start out by pretending to be someone you're not, or you risk forgetting who you are.

> I didn't want to smoke pot, but if I didn't he would think I was a real geek and not be interested in spending any more time with me. So I pretended to enjoy it and faked as best I could that I was inhaling the marijuana. But I felt real sick afterwards—sick from the smoke and sick from lying. I think I'll just avoid him from now on, if I can.
>
> Stacy, age 17

Be willing to end a relationship if it's not satisfying, if you believe it is causing you more harm than good, or if someone is asking you to give up yourself—your beliefs and desires.

Always remember you have the control to choose your friends. You don't have to be friends with anyone you don't want to be friends with. There are many, many people to choose from, and you will have opportunities to make new friends all your life. Explore the many diverse people around you and decide for yourself who makes a good friend for you. Finally, strive to create healthy friendships, but don't be too hard on yourself or others. No one is perfect.

Belonging

We all want to feel connected to others and to know that we belong. Many teens get a sense of belonging from being part of a group, club, or gang. When we become part of a group, we gain a sense of family. Having a group or gang to identify with is one way to overcome loneliness. Sometimes a group makes up for the love and support that is missing at home.

Common Ground: Overcoming Stereotypes

Often we choose our friends because we have things in common, such as shared beliefs, backgrounds, or race. But these similarities can also work to separate us from others. Many of us were taught that *different* is *bad*.

When we are afraid of or ignorant about differences, we sometimes stereotype people. A stereotype is an over-simplified or derogatory opinion about a group of people: "All people from New York are uppity"; "Boys only care about sex and sports"; "Gays are sick"; "Girls cry too much"; "All non-Christians are evil." Stereotyping some-one limits you and the other person. You won't be able to discover what someone is really like if you assume he is "bad," "stupid," or "evil." Stereotypes prevent us from enjoying all the different people around us. If you look past stereotypes you will find unique and interesting people.

With every person and group, you will find a common ground, if you choose. Finding a common ground does not mean we all become the same and believe the same ideas. Instead, we learn to appreciate the many differences between persons, groups, and nations. Our lives are enriched by these differences.

He looks downright bizarre. He wore clothes from his country—Ethiopia. And he was hard to understand when he talked in class. Then I met him at band practice. I wasn't too friendly at first, but it turns out he has a lot in common with me and some of my other friends. His favorite food is pizza. He likes to go for long bike rides. I admit that if I hadn't sat next to him in band I may never have found out how neat he really is. Another thing we have in common—we're both tall and hate basketball!

Paul, age 15

CHAPTER THREE

Family Relationships

We learn about ourselves and how we are expected to relate to others from our families. We seek acceptance and approval from our families in areas that are important to us, such as decisions, friendships, and sexuality. Our relationships at home can have both a positive and a negative effect on us, depending on how we are treated and how our parents treat one another.

What Do Your Parents Teach You about Relationships?
The most powerful method of teaching is by example. How your parents treat you and each other, what they say about others, and what their attitudes are about themselves have a deep and lasting impact on you. You may have learned some ideas about relationships that are not healthy or are simply outdated.

The longer and more often we behave a certain way, the more the behavior becomes a habit. Habits are hard to change. As a young adult, you have the time and opportunity to change some of your habits and outdated ways of behaving. But don't expect the people around you to support your changes or to change their own behavior. People only change their ways when they are ready—and no one can make someone else ready.

One group of teens got together and made a list of their parents' beliefs that they as young adults considered outdated. This list is not meant to imply that people who hold these beliefs are bad or ignorant. Rather, the list is a way to think about what you are learning from your family relationships. Which ideas do you agree or disagree with? Here is the teens' list:

- Boys and girls or men and women cannot be "just friends." Once you reach the dating age, your friends should always be of the same sex.

- If you are in a relationship with someone, you should spend almost all your time with this person—even at the expense of losing other friends.

- Men aren't expected to express their feelings; women aren't expected to be decision makers.

- Gays and lesbians can't experience true love or intimacy.

- When you commit to a relationship or marriage, it lasts forever, no matter what. You stay in a marriage

even if you and your spouse don't really love one
another. You pretend everything is okay when it's not.

▲ Divorce is always someone's fault, usually the husband's.

▲ There are some circumstances in which it is okay to
be physically or emotionally abused or to be abusive.

▲ Family issues or problems should not be taken outside of the home. The family can handle any crisis or
problem without outside help.

▲ Being alone (not in a relationship) is bad and weird.
You have to be in an intimate relationship to be happy.

▲ It is not nice to end a relationship. It's better just to
let things be, or quietly walk away without saying
anything. It hurts people's feelings to say good-bye.

▲ Boys have to pay for everything on a date.

▲ Mothers (women) are responsible for taking care of
family members' feelings; fathers (men) are responsible for the financial needs of the family.

▲ Boys can have sex as soon as they are old enough,
but girls should wait until they are in a committed
relationship.

▲ It's selfish to say no to family or friends who ask for
your help. Even if you can't or don't want to do something, it is better to say you will. Being selfish is bad.

▲ Girls' feelings are hurt more easily than boys! Boys
don't have as many or as intense feelings as girls.

The group identified these beliefs as outdated and began to develop new beliefs and behaviors for themselves. You can use this list to begin identifying any ideas you have been taught that seem right or wrong for you.

My mom always warns me about men. She says, "They just want to get your clothes off." She warns me not to give boys any idea that I like them physically. But I do like boys, only I'm really scared they are going to want to kiss or fondle me—and my mother would kill me if she found out! Sometimes I find myself hating boys too! Is sex all they want from me?

Amanda, age 16

My dad wakes me every morning at 5:00 and tells me to get used to working hard because that's what being an adult is all about. He always seems so angry with my mom—he yells at her all the time. If he's so unhappy, why does he work so hard?

Cody, age 17

My dad goes to my baseball games but once he's home all he does is watch TV. He never talks to me about anything, and I'm scared to approach him. I'm not sure what I would say to him.

Rick, age 15

I asked my mother one day if she thought I was pretty. She said no. She told me I was "different" looking and to be happy with that because my cousin who is beautiful is already having trouble with boys.

Julie, age 16

In these examples, the teens have learned a lesson about themselves and the world around them. One girl, Julie, is learning that she's not pretty in the eyes of others and that being pretty is not safe. She also gets the message that boys only care about "pretty" girls.

What can you do if you are learning habits and ways of relating to others that are either abusive or outdated? Even though the adults in your life still have authority over you, you can begin now to develop healthier patterns of relating to others. This doesn't mean you can expect others in your family to act in a new way, although that would be nice. More importantly, focus on yourself and the patterns that you want to change.

Healthy Families

Most families fall somewhere between being healthy and unhealthy emotionally. The less healthy our family is, the more we may need outside help to learn how to develop satisfying relationships. You could get outside help by reading a book, by talking to a counselor, friend, trusted adult, or relative, or by joining a group or social club.

How healthy is your family? Many traits make up a healthy family. These are some of them.

Needs are met. In a healthy family, your needs are acknowledged and attended to. You are provided with food, clothing, love, housing, and parental guidance.

Open conflict. Conflict is a natural part of any relationship. In a healthy family, conflict is a way to express and work out differences while trying to come to an agreement or understanding. Sometimes the understanding is simply an acceptance that we don't always agree. Conflict includes an open discussion of feelings and concerns.

My mom and dad ask that we air our arguments before dinner. One parent will ask my brother and me if there's something we need to talk about, or my brother or I will bring something up.

Last week I talked about how my brother comes into my room without knocking on the door first. I felt a little guilty about telling on him, but we worked it out.

Cheryl, age 14

Emotional openness. Emotions are part of every interaction we have with others. We are always feeling *something*, whether it is tired, content, sad, scared, numb, or embarrassed. In a healthy family, emotions are routinely expressed and respected. Feelings are expressed physically—for example, by crying, running around the block to work off anger, or giving someone a hug. Feelings are also expressed verbally—by talking to others about how you feel. In an emotionally healthy family, a wide range of feelings are allowed: sadness, happiness, anger, pride, embarrassment, courage, indifference, fear.

In an unhealthy family, often only one or two emotions, such as sadness or anger, are expressed. In many unhealthy families, any show of feelings is discouraged. It's important to express feelings in a way that is respectful to others. Instead of hitting or screaming, learn how to release and show feelings in a safe way.

Sexual boundaries are respected. Healthy families respect your need for privacy. Parents do not touch their children in a sexual way, and they teach their children not to touch their brothers and sisters sexually. Family sexual abuse, or incest, is against the law. Often, however, it is difficult to know what constitutes abuse. Any fondling or touching of your sexual body parts by a parent or any adult is against the law and is a serious violation of your rights. This includes french kissing, rubbing, intercourse, oral sex, and anal sex.

Other sexual violations are not always illegal but still pose a considerable threat to your health and well-being. If any of the following situations are happening to you, find an adult you can confide in safely.

▴ A parent or adult expresses a strong interest in your body and/or your sexuality. You have a right to privacy regarding your changing body and sexuality. Both parents should respect this privacy.

▴ A family member talks about sexual dreams or fantasies about someone else in the family.

▴ Someone "accidentally" touches you in a way that feels suspicious or sexual. For example, your father brushes his arm against your breast or thigh in a way that makes you uncomfortable.

▴ A family member gives you sexual hugs or kisses.

▴ A parent gives you an enema, suppository, or vaginal creams or insists that he or she help you with personal hygiene of any kind.

▴ Parents or older siblings walk around the house naked or partially dressed.

▴ Pornographic material, especially pornography that includes any form of sex with children, is accessible to you in your home.

▴ A parent uses vulgar sexual language.

▴ Adults have sex in front of you or within earshot.

▲ Adults or older siblings force you to be physically close to them when you prefer not to be. Healthy families respect that we don't always want to be touched. In fact, there are probably some people in your life that you would prefer not to have to touch at all. You should not be forced to touch anyone.

Individuality and autonomy. Healthy families acknowledge and encourage each person's uniqueness. Parents do not force their ideas on their children. Just because Dad gets up at 6:00 every morning to work and also works on Saturdays, he shouldn't expect his sons to have the same approach to work and money. Although Mom believes men are not to be trusted, her daughter should not have to live by this belief.

In a healthy family, differences and individuality are appreciated. No one feels, thinks, and behaves just like his or her parents. A healthy family accepts differences and doesn't make negative comparisons among family members.

My father has a wonderful way of helping me be proud of how I'm different from my sister. My sister is real good at a lot of things! My father reminds me that we all have talent, it just comes out in different ways and not always all at once. I finally discovered that I loved to play soccer, so my dad helps coach the team now. My sister comes to my games too when she has time.

Sue, age 14

Meaningful time. Meaningful time is a chance for family members to exchange feelings, ideas, and thoughts. It can be a playful time. An unhealthy family often doesn't know what meaningful time means.

I watch my mother fix dinner and sometimes she'll hear about something that happened to me that day. But my stories can't get too involved, because she's real busy fixing dinner for me, my two brothers, and my dad. She gets angry with me if I want to do something with her after dinner. She says I'm being selfish, and that we just spent a couple hours together while she prepared dinner. I often get a real bad stomachache after I eat.

Carrie, age 13

Carrie's mother doesn't know what meaningful time is. She assumes that the time she spends with her daughter while preparing dinner is enough. Carrie may come to believe that the little time her mother gives to her is all she deserves.

Spirituality. As a young adult, you may wonder about your place in the world and why you are here. A healthy family will encourage you to explore these questions. Some time is given to discussing issues of spirituality. Parents will help you think about the questions you might have about God, the problems in the world, or the meaning of life. A healthy family does not force you to accept certain beliefs or prevent you from exploring your own spirituality.

Authority. A healthy family has a flexible and clearly understood line of authority. The parents maintain discipline and guidance without being rigid or abusive. Family rules are reasonable and meaningful. In a healthy family, everyone is involved in decisions that affect the family. In an unhealthy family, one or both parents dictate decisions and do not ask for input from the children.

My dad always makes these plans for Sundays without checking it out with me. I'm 18 years old and I want to get together with friends or just stay home and read on some Sundays. But my father doesn't like it if one of us stays home. It wouldn't be so bad if he asked the rest of us what we want to do. Usually we end up over at his brother's house, and I baby-sit my uncle's eight-year-old.

Connie, age 18

Honesty. Healthy family members talk honestly with each other. In an unhealthy family, people lie and keep secrets. You may see your parents lying to each other, friends, employers, or neighbors. You may even be asked or told to lie and keep family secrets. If you learn to lie in your family, it will likely be difficult for you to be honest with others and trust that others are honest with you.

Changing What We've Learned

Twenty-five years ago, recycling garbage was not considered a priority in the United States. Americans believed that there was no end to our supply of resources and that throwing away plastic, cans, paper, and other waste was easy and safe. As you know, we can no longer live by these beliefs. Our planet is seriously endangered by human activities.

We as a society no longer support many ideas that were once considered "true" or "right." For example, many people once thought that slavery was justifiable, that women shouldn't be allowed to vote, and that gay people were mentally ill. Ideas about how we relate to each other, the environment, and ourselves all change over time.

A healthy society, family, or individual adapts to change. Being healthy means being willing to explore better ways of living. Giving up outdated and even harmful beliefs about how we live is difficult for many people. But part of growing up is adopting new and healthier ways of relating to the world and to one another.

New ways of relating to one another include breaking the silence and talking openly, not keeping harmful secrets, accepting differences, and having safe, healthy arguments. You do not have to keep family secrets about sexual abuse, alcoholism, drug abuse, or physical abuse. You don't have to carry outdated or harmful behaviors into your relationships. You can begin now to change your way of relating to your friends and family.

Often we carry unnecessary secrets, fears, and behaviors with us into our relationships. Growing up in an unhealthy family not only affects how you experience your childhood and teen years but influences what kind of adult you will be. If you are raised in an unhealthy family, you learn to doubt yourself and others. You might feel insecure and fear making choices.

During our young adult years, we can begin to discard unhealthy habits and try new ones. We can learn from our family experiences but we don't have to repeat them. Each of us is given opportunities to create our own life, including what kind of relationships we have with others.

You can become a teacher for your family through example. You cannot make anyone else change. You can, however, be an example of how a healthy person lives and behaves.

CHAPTER FOUR

Finding Love

The experience of romantic love in a relationship brings a wonderful sense of joy. Most of us seek an emotionally and physically intimate relationship at least once in our lives. Many people find love during their teenage years. Everyone deserves to have a loving relationship with another person.

Falling in Love

I know that when I am finished with school I will probably go to college. But the truth is that I still think a lot about finding the right guy.

Tricia, age 16

She's the most beautiful girl I have ever seen. Now if I could only get her attention.

Eric, age 17

I want to date, but I don't want all the fuss that goes with it.

Karl, age 17

I'm 18 years old, and I find myself only interested in dating others of my own sex. I don't have any way of knowing if other girls feel the same way.

Tess, age 18

When two people fall in love, many intense feelings emerge. The relationship may last a long time, or, more often during your teenage years, it may be a brief but meaningful experience. A relationship doesn't have to be long-term for it to be meaningful and loving.

Romantic love is intense. When you fall in love, it's natural to fantasize about the other person and what might happen between you. At the same time, it is important to separate your fantasy from reality. You may find yourself infatuated with a celebrity or someone you have only met once. These feelings are natural. Sometimes you become infatuated with someone who does not feel the same way toward you. This kind of disappointment can be quite painful.

Accept that many of your intimate relationships will be short-lived. Such acceptance can help you explore and enjoy what the relationship has to offer now, without worrying about making serious future plans.

Maybe you expect more from your boyfriend or girlfriend or the person you have a crush on than he or she can offer you. Other times, you might develop strong feelings for someone who doesn't turn out to be what you expected.

I always thought that if David ever got to know me he would fall in love with me. I spent most of my junior year finding ways to be near him. I went to every party that he went to. I expected to feel great once he noticed me and we started dating. I'd have someone special to go places with. But once we started dating, he mostly wanted to stay home and watch videos or go to parties. He didn't really have many interests other than that. Now I just want to tell him I'd like to go out with other guys, but I'm scared.

Janet, age 18

I hate it when she changes her mind and doesn't want to go out with me. It really hurts my feelings. We've been close for over a year, and we both believe we might be lesbians. Neither of us is interested in dating boys. I'm excited about the possibility of being romantic with her, but she sometimes freaks out and cancels dates with me. I want to call her up and scream and cry, but I know she needs time to work this out for herself.

Kris, age 19

You can't stop yourself from having intense feelings for someone, but you can decide how you will handle your feelings. You have choices. Learning to wait and focus your attention on other goals and activities will help you live with intense emotions without feeling compelled to do something about them.

Forcing an intimate relationship, like rushing a friendship, usually results in unhappiness. Real love and friendship don't have to be forced. You can't make someone like you or want to go out with you. All you can really do is tell the other person how you feel. Once you let the person know you're interested, get on with the rest of your life. If someone is interested in going out with you, he or she will let you know.

When you do get involved in an intimate relationship, you will probably feel a sense of belonging and completeness.

The "fit" will not have to be forced—you will not have to convince the other person to love you. Intimate relationships require commitment and compromise but should not be a constant struggle.

Being in an intimate relationship with the right person fulfills one of our deepest longings. We all want to connect with someone in a special way. It's worth waiting for the right fit before you commit to a long-term relationship.

Sexual Intimacy

Sexual exploration is a common and natural part of being a teenager. As a teen, you need accurate information about your changing body, your sexuality, and safe sexual behaviors. With the help of adults and peers, decide what your limits are before actually engaging in sexual activity with someone.

Although it is important to seek guidance from trusted adults, ultimately you will decide for yourself what your sexual limits are. What is acceptable to you? When you are on your own at a party or on a date, you'll have to rely on your own limits, not your parent's rules.

After you have decided what your limits are, discuss them with your boyfriend or girlfriend. Although it may be uncomfortable, talk before engaging in any sexual exploration. You don't have to feel pressured into trying something you aren't ready to do.

Exploration includes asking questions. How far do you want to go physically with your boyfriend or girlfriend? How important is it to you to be a virgin? How do you define virginity—no sexual contact whatsoever? What are you curious about? What sounds unappealing to you sexually?

How do you want to be touched? How don't you want to be touched? How do you feel about masturbation as a way to explore your sexuality? In summary, you might want to ask your boyfriend or girlfriend these additional questions as you become more sexually intimate:

1. What do you want/expect from me sexually?
2. Will you stop when I say stop?
3. If we decide to have sexual intercourse, will you be equally responsible for birth control?

If you choose to be sexually active, it's important to get information about safe sex, birth control, and sexually transmitted diseases. You also need accurate information about your developing sexuality. If you are unable or unwilling to get this information from your parents, consider approaching the health teacher at school, another trusted adult, or the school counselor.

When You're Feeling Jealous

When we have strong feelings for someone, at times we might feel jealous. Usually we feel jealous because we're afraid of losing someone we care deeply about. Our jealous feelings are a message that we feel hurt, scared, threatened, or ignored. All these reactions are natural. There's nothing wrong with feeling jealous—it's how we act on the feeling that sometimes leads to difficulties or harm.

I jumped out of my skin when I saw her talking with her old boyfriend. I know he still likes her. I wanted to punch him in the face and grab her away from him. It was scary having such strong feelings. I didn't do anything until I was alone with her and then I told her how I felt and asked her not to talk with him anymore. I was real pissed when she said she wanted to continue being his friend but she considered me her boyfriend. Well, I'm still angry and I'm not sure what I'm going to do about it.

Eli, age 17

Although Eli feels jealous of his girlfriend's friendship with her ex-boyfriend, Eli is trying to work it out with her. If he had acted on his initial feelings by punching the other guy in the face, he might have lost the chance to work it out with his girlfriend altogether.

When feelings of jealousy turn into behavior that is possessive, controlling, manipulative, abusive, or demanding, that's when we get into trouble.

I can't stand it if my boyfriend doesn't call me at night. I stay up all night worrying that he's with someone else. The next day I'm tired and pissed. I usually make him feel bad or angry about not calling me. I tell him that if he would just call I could get some sleep.

Katherine, age 16

Katherine will have many sleepless nights and arguments with her boyfriend if her sleep depends on his calling her. Her fear of losing him makes her act manipulative and possessive. There are many reasons why her boyfriend might not call her every night. She needs to change her expectations so she can sleep on nights when he doesn't call her.

Listening to our feelings is important. Sometimes feelings of jealousy reflect something that is actually happening—he *is* dating other girls behind your back or she *does* want to go out with other people. When we label certain feelings as "bad," we often feel ashamed to have them in the first place. The best way to deal with jealousy is to recognize the feeling and then do your best to communicate how you are feeling to others.

Are You Ready for Marriage?

Some people get married within the first couple of years after high school. As you know, marriage or another long-term commitment, such as living with your partner, is a serious decision that will affect many areas of your life for a long time.

Half of all marriages in the United States end in divorce. Divorce is often the best solution to marital problems—but perhaps many marriages should never happen in the first place. Sometimes people don't heed the warning signs or are unwilling to ask themselves a few tough questions before they get married.

If you are considering marriage (or any long-term commitment), the first question to ask yourself is why you want to get married. Why do you choose to spend the rest of your life with this person? Is this the best time in your life to commit to a marriage? Do you have other goals you want to accomplish before such a commitment? Are you afraid that if you don't get married now, the opportunity won't come again? Because so many marriages end in divorce, reviewing a list of reasons *not* to marry may be helpful.

Consider not committing to a marriage:

... if neither of you has a job or if you lack financial stability. Instead, consider waiting until you are financially secure and independent. Often one person (most often the woman) ends up financially dependent on her spouse and feels trapped in the marriage.

...if one or both of you are marrying to get away from your family. There are other ways to gain independence besides "running off to get married."

...if your future spouse abuses drugs or alcohol. Getting married will not make everything all right. In fact, marriage is stressful and takes a lot of work to make it a success. You deserve a partner who is mature enough to take on that responsibility. A person who abuses alcohol or other drugs probably does not have what it takes to be in a committed relationship.

...if you think that the marriage will change your partner or improve your relationship. If there are problems in the relationship before the marriage, they will still be there after the wedding ceremony. Often the problems actually get worse because you have such high expectations that things will improve after you're married. Marriage itself doesn't change people. Although people do change, to expect a specific change is risky. You are marrying the person you see *now*, just as he or she is.

...if you're in the middle of other major life changes, such as choosing a college, leaving home, or grieving a death in the family. These and other major changes deserve your full attention, just as the preparation for the wedding and the first years of marriage do.

. . . if you consider your family significantly unhealthy. Take time to learn healthy relationship skills before marriage. Most people who jump into a marriage without these skills will repeat their parents' problems. If your prospective spouse reminds you of the parent with whom you have the most problems, take this as a warning sign. Many people marry someone "just like" their troubled or abusive parent and end up regretting their decision.

. . . if something inside you says this might not be the right person or the right time for such a commitment. You probably feel hesitant for a good reason. If you marry with something bothering you, you may discover during the marriage why this person or time was not right for you. Perhaps you are also asking yourself if this person really loves you or if he or she is ready for such a commitment. These are important questions. Most often the answer to a question will come in time.

. . . if you fight a lot with your partner. No one can live happily in a relationship in which there is continual fighting and conflict. Constant fighting is usually a sign that you are trying to force something to fit that doesn't fit. The truth may be that your differences prevent you from getting along and that neither one of you wants (or intends) to change.

. . . if you aren't very good friends. If you don't seem to be friends, you won't make very good marriage partners either. The foundation for a healthy, loving, long-lasting marriage is a friendship.

. . . if your prospective spouse does not want to be monogamous. Monogamy means that both spouses are involved sexually and romantically only with each other.

. . . if you are getting married because someone is pressuring you. Base your decision on genuine feelings of love, rather than on pressure from anyone else. Sometimes people are encouraged to get married for reasons other than love and compatibility, such as wealth or attractiveness. Those things will not sustain a marriage.

. . . if the only reason you are getting married is that you or the other person is pregnant. A forced marriage between two people who otherwise would not get married is generally unwise. It is possible for both parents to be responsible for the child without getting married.

. . . if it is the only way your girlfriend or boyfriend will have sex with you. You have every right to want to be sexual, but to get married just to have sex does not create a very strong foundation for a lasting marriage. Consider safe sexual exploration without genital contact, or relieve your sexual urges through masturbation.

The healthiest relationships are made of all the ingredients that go into a friendship, plus monogamy and specialness. You and your romantic partner are *special* to one another. Your own mental, spiritual, and physical health must be a priority, but you'll also give much love and attention to your partner or spouse. Your partner deserves to be very important to you, and spending time with her or him will take time away from your hobbies, job, recreation, and parents. Unless you are ready to have someone be this important to you, you are not ready for a commitment such as engagement, living together, or marriage.

Consider holding off on marriage until you know you are ready. If you can't wait a few years to get married, ask yourself why. Chances are you are afraid about something. If you and your partner are meant to be together, a commitment can wait.

CHAPTER FIVE

Setting Limits in Relationships

We all depend on others to meet many of our needs. As a teen, you depend on your parents to provide you with food, clothing, and a safe, nurturing home. We depend upon one another for love, feedback, and support.

You've probably heard the term *codependency*. There are many definitions of the word. It was first used to refer to people who were in a troubled relationship with an alcoholic or a drug addict. Recently the idea of codependency has come to include a broad range of problems. Here's a simple definition of codependency: Codependency is focusing on someone else's behavior, feelings, and needs with little or no awareness of your own needs, feelings, and behaviors.

I learned about codependency in my Alateen meeting. I'm like many codependents who have an alcoholic parent. *I need to be needed.* My dad needed me to help him to bed when he was drunk, hide the booze from my mom, and find clean clothes for him in the morning when he was hung over. When he started to sober up and recover, I felt alone and unneeded, although I was happy to see him get better. Then I found myself getting involved with all sorts of people who needed me in some way or another—mostly to help them get out of trouble. I lent all my savings, even got hit in the face trying to protect someone else from getting hit. My Alateen group finally challenged me and said that unless I felt needed, I didn't feel loved. It's hard, but I am learning to get involved with people who can take care of themselves and don't need me to pick up after them.

Kristine, age 18

Codependency leads to a lack of self-awareness. As codependents, we forget our own feelings, thoughts, and needs when we are involved with others. Have you ever been with friends or on a date and found yourself too concerned about pleasing the others? Do you often lose sight of what you really feel or want in a given situation?

If you feel like you're too focused on others, you're not alone. Most of us are codependent to some degree. Sometimes we are taught not to attend to our own feelings and needs. We are told to put others first.

I can't let my grandma get hurt by my grandfather. He's real mean, so I decided to live with her until he dies. She needs someone to protect her and she's too old to defend herself.

Jason, age 17

What Jason is forgetting is that his grandmother has lived with her husband for over 40 years. Yet Jason is willing to give up his plans for college to protect her. Everyone needs help from others at one time or another. But each person is still responsible for his or her own behavior. When we take responsibility for other people's behavior, we take away their responsibility for themselves.

Being responsible for ourselves builds our self-esteem. When others always do things for us, we begin to feel that we can't take care of ourselves. This makes us feel inadequate and stupid. It is far more loving if we let others make mistakes—and sometimes even get hurt—than it is to protect them from the consequences of their decisions and actions. We learn from our mistakes and painful experiences.

We can love and care for others in ways that do not jeopardize our own health and well-being. When we give too much by "helping" someone, we become resentful.

> My sister is in a wheelchair. I love her and enjoy helping her. But my mother has taught me that it is just as important to take care of myself. She says that if I do too much for my sister, I may no longer enjoy the relationship. Sometimes I have to put myself first.
>
> Teresa, age 18

What's Your Bottom Line?

We all have our limits—our bottom line—of what we are not willing to give up or put up with to be in a relationship. Decide on your bottom line before entering a relationship. Here is a list of what one group of teens considered to be their bottom lines:

I will not be in a relationship with someone who:

▲ expects me to do things I consider dangerous

▲ hits me (or beats up on other people or animals)

▲ abuses drugs or alcohol

▲ is dishonest

▲ asks me to lie to my friends or family

▲ is rude to me and doesn't apologize

▲ pushes me to have sex when I don't want to

▲ isn't reliable; cancels plans without letting me know

▲ doesn't want me to spend time with my friends or family

▲ talks a lot about others behind their backs

Does this list include your bottom line? Can you add any of your own? Often our bottom line is very personal.

> I know this sounds strange to a lot of guys, but my bottom line is not to be criticized for what I'm into. I've been into designing and making clothes for the last two years and a lot of guys tease me about it. My uncle has been very successful in the clothing industry, and I don't find anything wrong with being successful. I've been told I have a natural talent for designing clothes. So if a friend can't accept and encourage this part of me, I don't need his friendship. That's my bottom line.
>
> Karl, age 19

It's important to draw your bottom line before you enter a relationship. Sometimes falling in love makes us blind to someone's destructive or harmful actions. Drawing a bottom line means caring enough about yourself to not let yourself be hurt or mistreated in relationships.

You might not want not to enter a relationship with

someone who expects you to be different from who you really are. If you have to change yourself for others, you may "lose yourself" or become unsure of yourself. You might get to the point where you wait for someone else to tell you how to behave.

Healthy Boundaries

In every relationship, you must establish and respect some boundaries. Our boundaries are what set us apart from others. Much as we use fences to separate our yards from other people's, we acknowledge boundaries in our relationships. A boundary is like a fence with a gate that leads in and out of your yard. Your friends should come into your fenced-in yard only if they are *invited*. If someone asks to come into your yard and you say no, he or she should respect you by staying outside the fence. The fence gives a clear message that people must be invited into your yard. Coming into your yard *un*invited is a violation. Some people may come in uninvited anyway—this is trespassing.

Personal boundaries are like this fence. People who force themselves on you without your complete approval are violating—trespassing on—your personal boundaries. Some personal violations are against the law, while others are not. No one has the right to violate any of your personal boundaries, however. Some personal boundaries include:

Physical boundaries: Your body belongs to you. No one has the right to abuse or mistreat your body in any way. Physical boundaries include how you want others to touch you or not to touch you. Physical boundaries create enough space between you and others that you feel safe and comfortable. Any form of physical abuse—kicking, hitting, biting, or whipping, for example—is a serious violation of your personal boundary and is also against the law.

Sexual boundaries: Sexual boundaries say to the world: "You can only be sexual with me by invitation." You must give your complete approval for someone to be sexual with you. Anyone who violates your sexual boundaries is breaking a law. This means you have the right to stop any sexual activity *at any time*. If someone continues after you ask him or her to stop, this is a violation.

Rape is forced sexual activity. Rape can occur between two people who have been dating for a while; even husbands have been arrested for raping their wives. Rape is a serious crime. No one has the right to force you to be sexual—ever.

Date rape is one of the most common forms of rape. It often happens after a boy and girl have dated a few times. Many young women do not report date rape because they feel responsible for it. They mistakenly believe that because they dated the young man, they somehow encouraged the attack. Some girls think that no one will believe they were raped because they knew their attackers. This is not true. Anyone who forces himself on you is breaking the law. Even if you "freeze" and don't fight back, it is still rape. (Feeling frozen or immobile during a rape is very common.) If you wonder whether or not you or a friend has been violated in this way, contact your local rape crisis center, which is listed in the phone book.

I asked him to stop kissing me. He was pushing too hard, and I didn't like it. We were alone and I was scared. Next time I'll go out with a group of people. It's safer and easier.

Carrie, age 14

Entering Relationships for the Right Reason

Ideally we do not enter relationships—friendships or intimate relationships—to build a sense of self-esteem. Instead, we need to go into a relationship with our self-esteem intact. Feeling good comes primarily from within ourselves, and relationships are a way to share good feelings with another person. When we start a relationship with low self-esteem, perhaps hoping that the relationship will boost our self-esteem, the relationship is likely to fail. It is not possible for someone else to make us feel better about ourselves consistently. That is too much to expect of anyone. If we depend on a relationship to make us feel good, we are codependent. Then if the relationship ends, our good feelings about ourselves might end too.

It's important to build your self-esteem, determine your bottom line, and set boundaries before you enter a relationship. You can easily get stuck in an abusive relationship or one that does not meet your needs because you feel that being in *any* relationship is better than being alone. This is not true. The times when you are not in an intimate, exclusive relationship can be very rewarding. During those times you might grow the most.

CHAPTER SIX

When It's Time to Say Good-Bye

Many teens remain in a relationship because they are scared to break up. Even if there are serious problems in the relationship, you might feel relieved that no matter what else is happening, at least you have someone to spend time with.

> I just kept getting together with him—even though we never did anything. I was so bored. Only this way I at least had someone who wanted to be with me.
>
> Jamie, age 16

Fear of being alone, fear of making new friends, or fear of how someone will react when you end a relationship are not good reasons to stay in any relationship.

When relationships fail to offer a mutual exchange of

companionship, respect, safety, and enjoyment, it is time to move on. It's okay to end a relationship. There are many reasons that you might want to end a friendship or romance:

▲ if it is abusive

▲ if you are the only one putting effort into it

▲ if your beliefs and values are *vastly* different from your friend's

▲ if you really don't care about or like the other person

▲ if you are being used for sex, money, or other gain

▲ if you are forced to act against your own values

Saying Good-Bye

When you decide to end a relationship, the following basic steps may help you:

1. Set some time aside to talk to the person (unless it is not safe for you) and actually say good-bye to one another. Tell each other why you are choosing to move on. Listen to one another's feelings.

2. Try to say the words "good-bye." "See ya later" is not the same as "good-bye." We often go to great measures to say anything but good-bye. But when it really *is* good-bye and not "till later," be honest with one another.

3. If you are changing the relationship somehow, from dating to friendship, for example, take time to talk about the new relationship. What does each of you mean by "friends"?

4. If you are ending an intimate relationship, seek the support of other friends and family. This is not a good time to isolate yourself. You may even want to join some kind of support group or social club.

5. Allow yourself time to grieve the relationship. You will probably feel sadness and anger that the relationship didn't turn out as you had expected or hoped.

6. Let go and move on. After the grieving period, get on with your life.

7. Begin to open yourself up to new relationships and experiences.

8. Take some time to reflect on the relationship. Did you do anything in it that you do not want to repeat in your next relationship? Were you treated in a way that was disrespectful or abusive? Have you come to discover a new bottom line as a result of this relationship?

You don't have to be in an intimate relationship to be happy. Similarly, being alone for a while is better than being in an abusive or neglectful relationship. You deserve to experience love, joy, and intimacy in all your relationships. When you end a relationship, you will experience the pain of separation and change, but this pain is not a message that you must be in a relationship in order to feel good.

Time Alone

"The man who goes alone can start today; but he who travels with another must wait till that other is ready."

Henry David Thoreau

Our society pushes relationships on us. Advertisements

make us feel we must be attractive to others—*"whiter teeth, fresher breath"*—and it often appears to be a "couples-only" world. Movies portray being alone as a devastating experience. Many people still believe there is something wrong with someone who is not married by the age of 30. The truth is, however, that being alone can be fun and a time of valuable personal growth. Learning to enjoy your own company makes periods of independence less scary.

You don't have to struggle to find an intimate relationship to feel good about yourself. There are many times throughout your life when being alone is the best thing. There are other times, especially when you're an adult, when being alone is forced on you by death, divorce, or a move to another state.

Whether you find yourself alone by choice or not, find interesting activities you can do by yourself. Treat yourself to a movie (yes, people attend movies alone), visit the zoo, or simply stay home and read a good book. You may even discover a new hobby or interest.

> I came to love Sundays. Even though I hated the idea of going to school the next morning, I had most Sundays to myself. I often baked my favorite cookies or read a book or wrote letters.
> Cyndy, age 17

Writing in your journal is a good way to have a conversation with a very interesting person—yourself! Remember, the most important ingredient in a healthy friendship is to be your own best friend. Spend some time alone and get to know yourself better so that you'll have a good foundation on which to build friendships and other relationships.

For Further Reading

Bell, Ruth, et al. *Changing Bodies, Changing Lives: A Book for Teens on Sex and Relationships.* New York: Random House, 1988.

Delisle, James. *Kid Stories: Biographies of 20 Young People You'd Like to Know.* Minneapolis: Free Spirit Press, 1991.

Espeland, Pamela, and Rosemary Wallner. *Making the Most of Today: Daily Readings for Young People on Self-Awareness and Self-Esteem.* Minneapolis: Free Spirit Press, 1991.

Johanson, Sue. *Talk Sex: Answers to Questions You Can't Ask Your Parents.* New York: Viking Penguin, 1989.

Johnson, Eric W. *Love and Sex in Plain Language.* New York: Bantam Books, 1988.

Johnson, Julie Tallard. *Celebrate You! Building Your Self-Esteem.* Minneapolis: Lerner Pub., 1991.

Larsen, Earnie. *Love Is a Hunger.* Minneapolis: CompCare Pub., 1979.

Rench, Janice E. *Teen Sexuality: Decisions and Choices.* Minneapolis: Lerner Pub., 1988.

_____. *Understanding Sexual Identity: For Gay and Lesbian Teens and Their Friends.* Minneapolis: Lerner Pub., 1990.

Rosenberg, Ellen. *Growing Up Feeling Good: A Growing Up Handbook Especially for Kids.* New York: Penguin Books, 1989.

Terkel, Susan Neiburg, and Janice E. Rench. *Feeling Safe, Feeling Strong: How to Avoid Sexual Abuse and What to Do If It Happens to You.* Minneapolis: Lerner Pub., 1984.

Varenhorst, Barbara B. *Real Friends: Becoming the Friend You'd Like to Have.* New York: Harper & Row, 1983.

If you have been raped, you can contact these places for help:
Rape/Crisis center or hotline
Community Mental Health Center
YWCA
Or dial 911.

INDEX

abuse, physical, 32, 40, 54, 56-57
abusive relationships, 18-19
alcohol, 25-26, 40, 48, 55

belonging, 28
boundaries, 56-57

codependency, 52-53
conflict, 34-35, 49
crushes, 42

date rape, 57
differences, 19, 29
divorce, 9, 10, 32, 47
drugs, 18, 25-26, 40, 48, 55

emotional support, 17, 35
ending relationships, 28; steps
    for, 60-61

feelings, 17, 35, 46-47, 53
friendship: early stages of, 27,
    28; qualities of, 15-21

gangs, 28
groups, 28

habits, 31, 34
healthy families, characteristics
    of, 34-39
honesty, 17, 39

incest, 35-37

jealousy, 45-47

love: falling in, 41-42; within
    a friendship, 19

marriage, 31-32, 47-51
monogamy, 50

parents, 30
pregnancy, 50

rape, 57
rejection, 26
reliability, 17, 55

secrets, 18-19, 40
self-esteem, 54, 58
sexual abuse, 35-37, 40, 57
sexual exploration, 44-45
sexuality, 44-45
shyness, 23-26
spirituality, 38
stereotypes, 29

threats, 19
time alone, 61-62
trust, 16

GARIBALDI SENIOR SECONDARY
24789 Dewdney Trunk Road
Maple Ridge, B.C. V4R 1X2